With love
from

_____

to

Nile

LITTLE ☆ STARS™

VIRGO

A parent's guide to the
little star of the family

JOHN ASTROP

with illustrations by the author

E L E M E N T

Shaftesbury, Dorset ● Rockport, Massachusetts
Brisbane, Queensland

© John Astrop 1994

Published in Great Britain in 1994 by
Element Books Ltd.
Longmead, Shaftesbury, Dorset

Published in the USA in 1994 by
Element, Inc.
42 Broadway, Rockport, MA 01966

Published in Australia in 1994 by
Element Books Ltd.
for Jacaranda Wiley Ltd.
33 Park Road, Milton, Brisbane, 4064

Printed and bound in Great Britain by
BPC Paulton Books Ltd.

British Library Cataloguing in Publication
data available

Library of Congress Cataloguing in publication
data available

ISBN 1-85230-542-8

CONTENTS

THE TWELVE SIGNS

Everyone knows a little about the twelve sun signs. It's the easiest way to approach real astrology without going to the trouble of casting up a chart for the exact time of birth. You won't learn everything about a person with the sun sign but you'll know a lot more than if you just use observation and guesswork. The sun is in roughly the same sign and degree of the zodiac at the same time every year. It's a nice astronomical event that doesn't need calculating. So if you're born between

May 22 and June 21 you'll be pretty sure you're a Gemini; between June 22 and July 23 then you're a Cancer and so on. Many people say how can you divide the human race into twelve sections and are there only twelve different types. Well for a start most people make assessments and judgements on their fellow humans with far smaller groups than that. Rich and poor, educated and non-educated, town girl, country boy, etc. Even with these very simple pigeon holes we can combine to make 'Rich educated town boy' and 'poor non-educated country girl'. We try to get as much information as we can about the others that we make relationships with through life. Astrology as a way of describing and understanding others is unsurpassed. Take the traditional meaning of the twelve signs:

Aries - is self-assertive, brave, energetic and pioneering.

Taurus - is careful, possessive, values material things, is able to build and make things grow.

Gemini - is bright-minded, curious, communicative and versatile.

Cancer - is sensitive, family orientated, protective and caring.

Leo - is creative, dramatic, a leader, showy and generous.

Virgo - is organised, critical, perfectionist and practical.

Libra - is balanced, diplomatic, harmonious, sociable, and likes beautiful things.

Scorpio - is strong-willed, magnetic, powerful, extreme, determined and recuperative.

Sagittarius - is adventurous, philosophical, far-thinking, blunt, truth-seeking.

Capricorn - is cautious, responsible, patient, persistent and ambitious.

Aquarius - is rebellious, unorthodox, humanitarian, idealistic, a fighter of good causes.

Pisces - is sensitive, imaginative, caring, visionary and sacrificing.

If you can find anyone in your circle of friends and acquaintances who isn't described pretty neatly by one of the above it would be surprising. Put the twelve signs into different lives and occupations and you see how it works. A Taurean priest would be more likely to devote his life to looking after the physical and material needs of his church members, feeding the poor, setting up charities. A Virgoan bank robber would plan meticulously and never commit spontaneous crimes. A Leo teacher would make learning an entertainment and a pleasure for her pupils.

So with parents and children. A Capricorn child handles the business of growing up and learning in a very different way to a Libran child. A Scorpio parent manages the family quite differently to an Aquarian. The old boast, 'I'm very fair, I treat all my children the same', may not be the best way to help your little ones at all. Our individual drive is the key to making a success of life. The time when we need the most acceptance of the way we are is in childhood. As a parent it's good to know the ways in which our little ones are like us but we must never forget the ways in which they are different.

LITTLE VIRGO

Little Virgo doesn't readily chuckle, beam and open arms to just any old person who smiles at them. They are a little more exclusive than that. Imbued with a natural modesty they always keep a respectable distance until absolutely sure whether whoever's making the advances is someone they want to know. The Virgo mind is as sharp as a tack and works incessantly, summing up every situation. It has to be like this for the Virgo drive is geared to keeping life running smoothly and perfectly on all levels. It's sometimes quite disconcerting to turn around and discover that for the last ten minutes you've been scrutinised, your activity assessed and recorded for information purposes to be recalled when the time is ripe. Often shy, they need plenty of closeness and support and no matter how much you admire their talents and praise them, never fear that it will go to their heads. Because of this, however, never think that it is not necessary. Far from it. It may seem from this that little Virgos are not going to be a barrel of

laughs. Wrong! Blessed with one of the sharpest minds in the zodiac and able to accumulate snippets of information at a startling rate, you will be followed around for the next few years by a completely entertaining little chatterbox. They won't share this pleasure with everybody, just their nearest and dearest, you lucky things! Rarely difficult to manage as young children, they not only fall easily into the family's household routines, they actually love them. For a little Virgo it's never too early to start helping Mom and Dad, for in tangible ways like this they gain the confidence they need so much. The ability to criticise also arrives prematurely, and once patterns of family behaviour are well established, deviation can cause undue consternation. Don't be surprised if you are scolded by this tiny tot for being ten minutes late for the start of nursery school. Learning to tell the time is one of the more important priorities for this little clockwatcher. Virgoan tidiness is renowned and if your babe has the habit, what bliss!; later on you're going to give the 'clear up that room' rows a miss. Even the less rigid Virgoan will have

a place for everything and have everything in it's place. I know a Virgoan artist whose studio is immaculate, tubes of oil paint, caps replaced, lined up in correct order of the spectrum from red to violet. The paintings are huge wild colourful abstracts though, just to surprise you. Just when you think everything about a Virgo is predictable you find the exception to the rule. They all have it. Something oddball that just doesn't fit. For this reason you'll find they have their fair share of great comedians, rock stars, inventors, and even crooks. Always with an underlying modesty though. Nice people!

THE BABY

Virgo babes usually like to start as they mean to go on, arriving on time and without too much fuss. Slow to give the smiles that other tinies hand out so readily, you could feel that the little eyes that twinkle as they follow your every movement

are giving you the once over before they commit themselves to a change in expression. Not the easiest of little ones in the first few months, they often seem to run the gamut of fretfulness, waking at the slightest noise or from tummy troubles. It seems as though they need a little bit longer than most to work out what the world is all about. They need all the stimulation that they can get for their bright, precise minds to take in; plenty of manipulative toys around the crib, such as beads, bells and mobiles will be preferable to large strange adults making boo boo noises a little too close. Real conversation will be appreciated even if you don't think they can possibly know what you are talking about; you can never be sure. Small Virgos start making their first words early but, as with most things they do, you'll hear them practise on their own before they try it out on you.

THE FIRST THREE YEARS

Most of the stages in early growing up can get a little delayed not so much because little Virgos are really slow but more because of their dread of not quite getting things right. They'll keep you feeding them purely because they hate the mess they made at the first attempt. A great deal of reassurance and positive praise will help. You can't overdo it with this one. None of this is really worth worrying about anyway for as soon as they feel they're ready to move on to the next milestone of development they'll do it just that bit better than other children of the same age. Your small Virgo will never seem to be totally at home with aunts and uncles who insist on sitting him on their laps and making a fuss of him. In the first couple of years they get quite adept at wriggling free of this humiliation. No hearty ribtickling will turn the apprehensive little face into chuckles. Life is serious and has to be understood and sorted out before we start any fooling around. Despite this natural reserve, little Virgos need lots of reassurance.

Actions for them speaking louder than words, it's what you do together that matters rather than what you say. Practical activities that can be shared, simple games and small chores, become a marvellous way to ease the situation. From the earliest  days Virgos love lists of anything, word books with masses of pictures each with it's name will be remembered meticulously. The ability to recall car names, flowers, football teams, whatever takes their fancy, will amaze you. They are the best of company for themselves but may need some help with making relationships by frequent visits from little playmates. The gentler ones, at first, anyway!

THE KINDERGARTEN

Thrown straight in at the deep end, this sudden new experience can be quite traumatic for little Virgo. Although rarely making big scenes she may become withdrawn if not supported in gradually getting used to the hurly-burly of a boisterous nursery school. Usually preferring just one little friend to travelling round from chum to chum, encouragement to invite home her closest companion will help considerably in the early days. Although so young, the true Virgo role of helping others will start to show and your little one will soon find the

confidence to help teacher tidy up the debris at going home time. Other new, even less secure children will be assisted and made happier by your little soul's kindness. The Virgo confidence grows when they feel they are being useful.

School and Onwards

Having gained the experience of kindergarten the change to a real school will be almost welcomed. Where learning has become the important activity little Virgo can excel. Bright- minded with an excellent memory for facts and figures and an orderly approach to school routine, it would be hard to keep a typical Virgo from the top of the class. During the all important first years your young protégé's confidence should grow, as often during this time small responsible jobs will fall on this conscientious child's shoulders. Virgos make the best monitors and prefects later on with their

modest ways, maintaining friends in both camps – the class and the teachers. At this time the food fads may start to show. Always somewhat picky, these little fusspots may just insist that school lunches are a complete no-no. Even your packed lunches have to be just so. Diet and health are a Virgoan obsession, many becoming vegans at quite an early age, and rarely will you find an overweight gourmet, among the young ones at least. Nouvelle cuisine must have been a Virgo creation. The least of your worries will be the learning. They are great achievers and in the quietest way will usually maintain their top position throughout the school years.

THE THREE DIFFERENT
TYPES OF VIRGO

THE DECANATES

Astrology traditionally divides each of the signs into three equal parts of ten degrees called the decanates. These give a slightly different quality to the sign depending on whether the child is born in the first, second or third ten days of the thirty-day period when one is in a sign. Each third is ruled by one of the three signs in the same element. Virgo is an Earth sign and the three Earth signs are Virgo, Capricorn and Taurus. The nature of Earth signs is basically practical so the following three types each has a different way of expressing their practical abilities.

First Decanate - August 24 to September 2

These are the Practical Perfectionists. This is the part of Virgo that is most typical of the sign qualities. They are down-to-earth and quick thinking with an excellent critical sense. Because of the latter they tend to be fastidious in dress, food, and work matters. Many achieve their success in later life in areas where this ability to analyse and sift the best from the ordinary is of great use. Their perfectionism is partly responsible for their modesty and most spend their lives believing that everything they do could be just that little bit better. For this reason, many young Virgos from this decanate do especially well in school and achieve distinction (in Virgo terms) for their outstanding efforts in adult life. Teaching and caring – two of the Virgo attributes – are well represented in Maria Montessori and Mother Teresa, both going out of their way to avoid unwanted publicity for their splendid work. Although there are a fair share of these Virgos in showbusiness they seem to function best in a directing, producing role and even though many of them achieve great acclaim it is in their background role that they earn their most fulfilling successes.

Second Decanate - Sept. 3 to Sept. 12

This is the Ambitious Perfectionist. Although still sharing the quiet modest attributes of the typical Virgo, those born at this time are less reluctant to serve their cause by stepping into the public eye. Great patience is available in any cause that they deem sufficiently important and sometimes many years of painstaking work goes into their achievements. They are blessed with accurate and witty observation powers in all that they see around them which they are able to assimilate, adapt and use creatively in furthering their careers. Often children born in this decanate will have an extra-serious approach to life when they are quite small and may need a little more help learning to relax and have fun. This, however, seems to gradually wear off as they get older, when they will often seem to be half the age of their contemporaries both in looks and attitude to life in general. More ambitious than the other two decanates, they are aware that good connections are all important to help them achieve their aims and for this reason they always seem to make powerful friends. They are usually strong traditionalists, supporting authority and the status quo.

Third Decanate - Sept. 13 to Sept. 23

The Artistic Perfectionist. This is not to say that Virgo artists only come from this part of the sign, but here they are ruled by the planet Venus giving an altogether softer and more pleasure loving quality to the otherwise thrifty and rather frugal

Virgoan approach. There is also a strong link with the Taurean enjoyment of the good things of life and the talent for taking something quite ordinary and seemingly worthless and turning it into something of value. They are usually good in business and well able to make their way in life successfully in a material sense. Although most Virgos are careful, if not obsessive, with diet, the latter third of Virgo is where surprisingly enough you may find more than a few bon viveurs. Despite the fact that skinny little Twiggy, the cult model of the swinging sixties, fits the earlier description, Mr Cadbury blessed the world with chocolate bars, and the great B.B. King, who turned simple folk blues into an enormous popular following, always looks delightfully like a man who knows what he likes and gets plenty of it.

OTHER LITTLE VIRGOS

Mums and Dads like you delighted in bringing up the following little perfectionists. Yours will probably turn out to be even more famous!

First Decanate Virgo

Aubrey Beardsley, Leonard Bernstein, Samuel Goldwyn, Lyndon Johnson, Johann Wolfgang von Goethe, Ingrid Bergman, Richard Attenborough, Richard Gere, Rocky Marciano, Sean Connery, Mother Teresa, Maria Montessori, Edgar Rice Burroughs, J.A.D. Ingres.

Second Decanate Virgo

Richard the Lionheart, D.H. Lawrence, Leo Tolstoy, O. Henry, Arthur Koestler, Sonny Rollins, Louis MacNeice, Harry Secombe, Arnold Palmer, Freddie Mercury, Jesse James, Peter Sellers, Maurice Chevalier, Anne Seymour, Raquel Welch.

Third Decanate Virgo

Tintoretto, Lauren Bacall, Stirling Moss, Ann Bancroft, Queen Elizabeth I, Dick Turpin, Roald Dahl, B.B. King, Twiggy, Greta Garbo, Stephen King, H.G. Wells, Jacqueline Bisset, Gustav Holst, Michael Faraday, George Cadbury, Brian Epstein, Sophia Loren, Tommy Lee Jones, Agatha Christie.

AND NOW THE

PARENTS

THE ARIES PARENT

The good news!

The Aries parent is a strong but generous authority figure in home life and little Virgo is happiest with a firm, well-established pattern within which to grow and improve. Young Virgos learn quickly with great application and modest devotion, sifting and analysing with their sharp little minds each new piece of information. Aries parents, no lovers of routine, may find themselves organised and co-opted into regular appointments for games and educational assistance. The Virgoan love of facts, figures and good hard work can leave little Virgo on the fringe of the fun but the Aries parent will encourage friendships and help shy young Virgo find independence. Good little organisers like these are invaluable in group situations but unlike Leos, they wait to be  asked. Often wishing they could be as forceful and positive as you, your small Virgoan will nevertheless gain strength from the partnership by being able to give you tangible help. Always make it something practical: sorting out the nuts, bolts, nails and screws in the tool cupboard, putting the family photo album in order, these are things at which the youngest of Virgoans excel. They'll always be proud of you so let them do something that will make you proud of them. Never fear that little Virgo will get big-headed. These children are usually whizzkids at games, especially the mental type. Your natural competitive instinct should find quite a challenge when playing Scrabble and word puzzle games. In the early days it would be nice if you lost a few times, later on you'll have a job not to. A few chess grand masters come from this part of the zodiac.

...and now the bad news!

Conflicts can arise if Aries is too ambitiously pushy on Virgo's behalf. Yes, this child will be bright and a credit to you, but very few Virgos like taking centre stage. The fear of being propelled into anything risky or potentially embarrassing will evoke sharp criticism and pointed sarcasm that can deflate even an Aries ego. The smallest ones can nag like an adult: 'you should've', 'why didn't you?', 'wouldn't it be better if you'. The negative side of this partnership will come into full being if you don't allow little Virgo plenty of preparation for even the simplest journey. 'Spontaneous' is not in the Virgoan vocabulary. Fair warning is of the essence; they'll let you know when they're ready – in triplicate.

THE TAURUS PARENT

The good news!

Little Virgos are bright and intelligent, with a love of getting things right that puts them high in the ranks of quick learners. Calm Taurus has a similar down-to-earth liking for order and will respect and encourage young Virgo's neat virtuosity. Little will ruffle the smooth running of this relationship. Junior is just as hungry for knowledge and know-how as Gemini, but has the advantage of being a little more thorough. If anybody likes thoroughness it is you, Mr or Mrs Taurus. There'll be questions galore for the patient Taurean parent to answer, plus, would you believe, note-taking. Virgos back up their good memories with copious notes, lists, and schedules almost as soon as they can write ABC. Junior's natural reserve and conscientious application to work can make for shyness and difficulty in relating to others. Little Virgo will need warm but unobtrusive encouragement in order to build the confidence to 'mix'. If you can help to establish one or two friendships for this modest little one, then you have done your job well.

In his gang of little contemporaries don't expect to see your protégé taking the lead, but he will rarely be bashful in reminding his buddies of the rules of the game every now and then, just to make sure things run smoothly. Routine which you both thrive on will be great fun if you can share with little Virgo some of the practical chores. The best way for her to gain confidence is by seeing positive results of her labours. The traditional picture of little boy or girl up to the elbows in flour and pastry helping Mom is great, but when it's with a Virgo child they make real cakes and you'll like 'em. Next week it'll be raspberry cheesecake.

...and now the bad news!

There is hardly any way in which this relationship should go wrong but the usual one is Taurean obstinacy coming up against a nagging supercritical Virgoan. Yes, little Virgoans can turn into the family critic telling just about everybody how and what they should be doing. And let's face it, Taureans do sometimes insist on sticking out against all odds that their system is right. The resulting standoff will have young Virgo turning into a bag of nerves and getting even pickier about her food. It's funny how all family arguments with a Virgoan, big or small, seem to end up with a dietary problem. Could be the Virgo secret weapon!

♊

The Gemini Parent

The good news!

Geminis have no trouble in creating a stimulating environment in which any child can flourish. Little Virgo has a bright, responsive mind, quick to grasp new ideas and put them to practical use. This ease of learning soon makes this relationship strong in terms of communication. Although mentally a perfect match for this intelligent parent, young Virgo's drive takes a different route. Establishing modest but efficient patterns and routines gives this youngster self-confidence and security.

Often painfully shy, little Virgos can take unlimited praise for effort without becoming in the least big-headed. Don't make the mistake of thinking that it isn't necessary though. That matter of fact manner belies the need for a fair share of Gemini hugs and kisses. The sociable aspect of your life should be a great assistance to little Virgo who needs plenty of encouragement to meet new people and make new friends. This will be a slow process, however, for unlike you, your little chatterbox will prefer very few friends and may go silent on you when put into

too large a group situation. Often the Virgo confident use of words shows itself quite early as a talent for writing and this will be a delight to any Gemini parent. An old beat up type-writer could be the start

of something big. Note the number of really good crime writers who are Virgos. In fact this is typical of the way in which the Virgo mind works away at a problem, picking up each clue, turning them over in the mind and sifting through until only one answer can be the correct one! What a bore! Never did like those stories, not fast enough for a Gemini! There will be times when roles get reversed and this child will be working hard to keep parent interested enough to finish a shared project. They'll nag you. Yes, little Virgo will sometimes be a touch too thorough and more than a little on the conventional side for your own taste, but anything for the kids eh!

...and now the bad news!

This child's respect for reason and authority makes clashes almost non-existent. However, Gemini's sometimes scattered and unpredictable enthusiasms can put too much on Junior's plate for comfort. If you don't want a supercritical nervous wreck, let little Virgo finish one job before starting the next. The other danger is that you'll be just too busy to notice anyway. Even if they're pining away from lack of... you name it.... the little Virgo will rarely complain. Not equipped with a Leo's roar or Piscean floods of tears, no fuss, no bother, no tantrums, this poor little fellah just keeps it quietly to himself and picks at his food and doesn't really fancy anything at the moment thanks Mum, no I think I'll just have a lie down for a while. Yes, Virgos can, very very modestly, get you where it hurts!

THE CANCER PARENT

The good news!

You are a loving and protective friend and have a natural feeling for parenthood. The Virgo child is a quick learner and has the innate ability to work hard at things in order to get them right. Cancer parents never forget their own childhood pleasures and difficulties and are able to sense when and where not to help. Little Virgos are seldom troublesome, enjoy being given small responsibilities, and take pride in doing their best. The Cancer parent will not be critical (the Virgo's love of perfection hates mistakes) but will quietly help when things go wrong. Virgos can be constant worriers if made to feel they are not coming up to scratch. Cancer can dish out large helpings of encouragement and admiration and it won't go to the head of this modest little one. The most important Cancer addition to little Virgo's matter-of-fact repertoire will be imagination. Your ability to conjure up and visualise fantasy situations and games may sometimes get a puzzled look or a blunt retort from your tiny realist. Seeing the world in practical terms is the Virgoan way of feeling secure, so while increasing the child's imaginative abilities you may have to explain just how the magic carpet works, how the frog can change into a

prince and if the goose lays golden eggs where does it make its babies? Never as hyperactive but certainly as inquisitive as a Gemini child, you will have to face a continual barrage of questions. The Cancerian love of accumulated bygones, diaries, old encyclopedias and photo albums should be a paradise for this constantly curious child. Encouragement to assist you in keeping a diary of events and making sure that your calendar is up to date will develop little Virgo's sense of routine and order and be a great help to you. When this child helps a parent it needs to be real and not just a game.

...and now the bad news!

Occasionally problems with this relationship can occur because of the differences in the two sign qualities. Cancer can be quite overprotective and for this reason give way to the sometimes obsessive nature of little Virgo. Virgo's love of perfection and order, allowed to become compulsive by a doting parent, may produce a super- critical nature that finds fault with everything and everybody. People can stand just so many 'you shoulds'. Cancer's gentle humour and ability to send-up without malice may help. The serious Virgoan is made even more perfect with a good measure of laughter added. If possible, a pet of some kind can also warm that often cold seriousness, expanding the caring nature; they love the responsibility and won't neglect any little creature that's in their charge.

♌

THE LEO PARENT

The good news!

Your motto, if you're a typical Leo parent, is 'big · is beautiful'. Leos, who always operate on a large scale, may find it hard at first to understand the Virgo child's preoccupation with accuracy and detail. Little Virgo likes to get a thing right even if it takes a lifetime to do so. This child's critical faculties are unparalleled, finding the proverbial needle in the haystack at a speed which can stagger the laissez faire attitude of the easy-going Lion. Young Virgos carry out their tasks conscientiously and precisely. That's where their particular talents lie. Accuracy to them is far more important than success, recognition, or applause, and they work more happily behind the scenes than in the spotlight. Leo, who needs a pat on the back to get by in life, may puzzle over shy young Virgo's humility, but it is this very modesty, this willingness to work and serve without recognition that represents real strength. Your home, as with all Leos, will be comfortable and provided with everything that this youngster could wish for. Some people would say that you spoil your children but you, with your natural generosity, would see giving the best you could afford as a necessity. Much attention will be put into providing creative

stimulation and encouragement for your little
Virgo but it must be remembered that the Virgo
pace is nowhere near as enthusiastically driving as
the Lion's. In fact you may be disappointed not to
find your verbal enthusiasm reflected in your small
perfectionist, her common sense tells her that all
that stuff gets nothing done and only a concen-
trated attention to the creative matter in hand will
get things right. Leos are proud people and need
to take pride in their children. Little Virgo's power
behind the throne qualities will become apparent
and appreciated as the true worth of this modest
little helper is understood.

...and now the bad news!

As with most adjoining signs the differences
are great and clashes can sometimes occur. If Leo's
enthusiasm manifests in a domineering, pushing
way, as a means of defence this youngster's critical

tendency may sharply point out faults that are a little hard to swallow. Leo dignity won't take criticism easily from such a cheeky little whipper-snapper and if they get into word battles guess who's going to come off worst! No, avoid this one, for the best of warm-hearted Leo's nature can, with tolerant affection, develop young Virgo's discriminating rather than nit-picking nature. Your sometimes over-the-top generous nature can worry thrifty little Virgo if you press him to be the same. The best that you can do is hit a middle-of-the-road balance between the two of you and love each other for the differences.

♍

THE VIRGO PARENT

The good news!

How lovely to have a little like mind in the family. You are a happy, orderly, bright-minded duo, and the conversations, once Junior's mastered the language (and that's usually pretty quickly), will be sparkling. Little Virgo is just bubbling with insatiable curiosity to know every fact and figure about the world around. What can't be stored in the mind will later fill neat notebooks and files. Just like the Virgo parent, this youngster is here to get some semblance of order and system out of this messy old world. A perfect relationship between two per-fectionists! Well we may just find that too much of a good thing may leave Junior with the idea that the rest of the world are inefficient slobs. Mum or Dad Virgo have learnt that it takes all sorts to keep the wheels turning and it could be well worth passing that on to little Virgo before beautiful friendships are broken with the jab of a super-critical tongue. However, modesty usually prevails, to the extent that these little ones can become self-effacing and painfully shy. A few well selected friends round to tea on a fairly regular basis can

do much to develop confidence in this area. Parent and child show love and affection in practical ways and encouraging Junior to help you will expand feelings of closeness. The real quality that you both share is the need to give the best possible perform- ance in the service of others and everything that you do in terms of seeking perfection is fulfilled by that simple means. This sounds dreadfully dull but a Virgo comedian getting the timing just right every time and giving the right kind of gag for the right kind of audience sometimes gets the laughs a great deal better than a showy Leo saying 'look how funny I am everybody'. Wasn't Peter Sellers great at this?

...and now the bad news!

What can go wrong with the two of you always trying to get everything done in the best of all pos- sible ways? Well for a start you can drive everyone else in the household and the near vicinity absolutely mad!!! There is little chance that you'll find anything but easy agreement on how the world could be put right. Your tidy minds may just have to let up a little on less well-ordered souls, especially if you've some in your own family. Virgo nagging is renowned and although we all secretly love to be attended to by devoted Virgos dusting the dandruff off our jackets and tutting when we leave our books and magazines all over the living room – but two of you...need I say more?

♎

THE LIBRA PARENT

The good news!

For an easy-going Libran you may find little
Virgo a bit on the stiff and starchy side until you
discover that what your tiny fusspot is looking for
is just a bit more system and practicality in her life.
Little Virgos like to know where they stand with
regards to everything every minute of the day, and
if possible they like to know an hour ahead of time
just to be on the safe side. Not the hardest problem for a laid back Libran to deal with, your
sociability will win where all else fails. Virgo and

Libra are both mentally active and communicative and parent and child should have plenty to say to each other. Lots of talk from the earliest years will build a good rapport between you both. Often reserved and shy, little Virgo, in this sociable parent's company, will be able slowly to develop the confidence to feel comfortable with others. The easy-going Libran may find Junior's preference for regular routines and predictable patterns of behaviour somewhat limiting but worth adapting to for

the self-reliance that follows. Little Virgo's careful attention to details makes for quick learning and once school is started the end of term reports can be a delight. Discipline is never a big problem with these conscientious youngsters as

they are prepared to provide most of it themselves. This relieves the Libran parent of having to become a firm authority figure, a role that doesn't fit too well on the shoulders of such a peace lover. Rarely comfortable with showy displays of affection, and often undemanding in this area, Junior prefers to show love in practical ways. Being allowed to help Mom and Dad has double the meaning to this little one. Although your little one sometimes may seem indifferent to demonstrative shows of love, never believe that they don't need quite as many hugs and kisses as more outgoing children.

...and now the bad news!

The other side of the Virgo coin is not so pretty a picture. Without positive help and encouragement to learn the Libran art of relaxing and taking it easy, this child can become obsessively fussy, finicky, supercritical and a constant nag. All work and no play, you know the rest. You may find as school becomes more important, that the desire to do well can become too much of a pressure and tempers (very quietly) fray. Here you will have to use all your diplomacy to help keep the balance just right for this conscientious little worker. Arrange plenty of trips out and lots of socialising, as long as Junior is not pushed too much to the fore in group activities. He's going to come way up near the top of the class anyway!

♏

THE SCORPIO PARENT

The good news!

You're fascinated by people and love to get insights into their deepest secrets; you like to know what makes people tick. For this reason Scorpios usually make quite good natural psychologists which is, of course, a great asset in bringing up children. The perceptive Scorpio parent will soon discover little Virgo's delightful mental agility. Sharp as tacks, quick to learn and even precocious in their skilful orderliness. With this little one, Scorpio can lock away the powerful discipline (Junior's own is perfectly adequate) and bring out the love and affection. Small Virgos read, question and talk, filing away the information in the tidy pigeon holes of their bright minds. A place for everything and everything in its place builds Junior's self-confidence. Scorpio's almost psychic understanding of other people's strengths and weaknesses will be invaluable support for this modest Virgo. The

expression of feelings in a child that dislikes show and pretension will need gentle coaxing but never smothering affection. Though happy in play, little Virgos are happiest when applying themselves to projects with good tangible

end results. Helping Mom and Dad with 'real' jobs will be enjoyably constructive, for in this practical way they can find it easiest to express their love. Little Virgos, although more reserved than some other children, will have their share of talent. Modesty in no way deprives us of great abilities and many Virgos quietly shine way above their fellows. Scorpios are born entrepreneurs, the stuff that great impresarios are made of, and if they spot talent in their beloved child they'll nurture and help her to develop, always of course staying well in the background. This child will respond far better to being a vital part of a team rather than going it completely alone, so work together, project for project, for the best results.

...and now the bad news!

Family clashes should be minor in this relationship, with little to arouse Scorpio's sometimes quick temper. The emotional outbursts of Scorpio will be very hard for this less demonstrative child to understand and may well cause greater consternation than you would expect if and when they occur. Little Virgo, although devoted to working hard on any projects that you may plan for her, will never be able to manage the enormous challenges that you would choose for yourself. It may be as well to look at yourself occasionally and see whether you are pushing your small Virgo into bigger things than she is able to manage well. It would be sad to push this little perfectionist into a quite undeserved failure. Breaks of routine for Junior are not always taken easily and may sometimes cause a sharp critical response. Help this little one to learn that occasionally bending and even breaking the rules adds a little fun to life.

THE SAGITTARIUS PARENT

The good news!

You are probably one of the most adventurous characters in the zodiac. Your love of long-distance, free-ranging travel both mentally and physically stays with you throughout your enthusiastic life. Your little Virgo has none of this and doesn't think as big as you, in fact, tiny would be infinitely preferable for this i-dotting and t-crossing little perfectionist. So where's the link between the two of you? Parent and child, though widely different in temperament, have a mutual respect for the truth that should make for close companionship. Sagittarius's friendly, straight from the shoulder honesty, and kindly tolerance, fits well with little Virgo's love of the plain unvarnished facts. Now for even more differences. Fun-loving Sagittarian mums and dads like to be free as birds, hate ties and are rarely happy with routine. Small Virgos have their feet on the ground, like to know the limits and thrive on routine. A big contrast, but in no way irreconcilable once recognised. Junior's need for firm guidelines and familiar patterns will, if supported, develop into an early self-reliance that makes few demands on this freedom-loving parent. Little Virgo's insatiable interest in getting the facts

and Sagittarius's mine of information make good conversation the mainstay of this relationship. The Sagittarian impulse to propel themselves recklessly into new experiences will not be shared by this cautious child. If Junior's coming along for the ride, make plans and make sense. Little Virgos are great organisers, and this talent can be given a boost if Sagittarius encourages help in drawing up the itinerary and mapping the route. The reward is high if the risks are kept low.

...and now the bad news!

The most prevalent problem between these two signs is the blunt honesty of the Sagittarian tongue coupled with the reserve and retiring nature of Virgo. The latter gets hurt easily and the Sagittarian, usually so busy and on the move, can easily overlook the unwitting devastation they have caused. In the nicest possible way the Archer tells everything like it is. If they think you're a lazy fat slob they'll greet you with, 'Hi fatso, isn't it about time you did a little work and got rid of that spare tyre?' Subtlety is not in the Sagittarian book and if little Virgo is ever on the receiving end of an indelicate remark he can go into a quiet sulk for weeks. The Virgo secret weapon in retaliation for most injustices is to start having problems with diet and food matters. At the drop of a hat this one can become a vegan with a hearty dislike of vegetables and a wan, hurt expression that indicates that the worries of the world are on those little shoulders.

♑

THE CAPRICORN PARENT

The good news!

This is an almost too good to be true meeting of like minds and everything else. Both Earth signs, Capricorn and Virgo will get a great deal of enjoyment from each other's company, having in common a healthy respect for the practical, material aspects of life. In the secure support of this parent the little Virgo's bright inquisitive mind will develop quickly and confidently. Always ambitious for their children, the Capricornian parents spend unlimited time and patience on their little charges.

However perfect they may seem to this parent, the extreme modesty of small Virgos will need plenty of enthusiastic encouragement to boost a sense of self-worth. It's all too easy to overlook this necessity when Junior's self-discipline works so well. Often finding it difficult to express affection in other than helpful practical terms (doing little jobs for Mum and Dad) the desire to receive hugs, kisses, and compliments is powerful, but if you don't give them, they won't ask. Little Virgo's a

talker, and from the earliest days good conversation will be an important key to this relationship. Overindulged in their perfectionist natures these little ones can be infuriating fusspots, picky eaters, and harsh critics. Soften yours up with large doses of love and tomfoolery. Capricorns are always ambitious for themselves and also for their children. Both of you see life as a serious matter and get a great deal of satisfaction in mastering and putting into order the chaos of everyday life. There may be times, however, when the introduction of more fun-provoking projects would do the two of you a great deal of good. This is where little Virgo has a chance to develop some of the natural Virgo wit that's just waiting for release. The Virgoan use of words is outstanding and it would be a shame if these were only devoted to humdrum everyday matters. There are a lot of comedians and comedy scriptwriters amongst the Virgo clan.

...and now the bad news!

Well there's hardly any with you two! But... as we nearly said above, the all work and no play routine of two solid Earth signs can get to be a bit of a bore. It's even worse for us other signs if you don't notice it! There's a funny thing about Capricorns, although very serious in the earlier part of their lives, later on they get more and more relaxed and start having real fun when the rest of us are just about giving up. Have a heart. Little Virgo won't be able to do this like you, so make sure he or she gets a good dose of the fun right now!

THE AQUARIUS PARENT

The good news!

The Aquarian parent provides plenty of stimulation and excitement to keep the zippy little Virgo's intellect busy. The infectious spontaneity and amusing originality of Aquarius can contribute much towards easing the sometimes excessive modesty and caution of this little perfectionist. However, the Virgoan desire for order and system may not react so favourably to the constant change of routine that is second nature to the freethinking Aquarian. Much as you love complete freedom, disliking ties of any kind, little Virgo's self-assured independence will more than repay you sticking to repeat patterns of family behaviour. Within such a good predictable structure Junior can get on, unhampered, with the business of becoming better and better (at everything). The need to be helpful and turn their talents to practical use makes young Virgos take on responsibilities far in advance of their years. As they usually prefer to express their love in the same practical way,

helping Mom and Dad takes on extra meaning for them. Plenty of praise for jobs well done is essential to build self-confidence and there is no chance of modest little Virgo getting big-headed. The Aquarian mind is good at taking a set idea, turning it on it's head and challenging the traditional view. In fact this is the basic drive of the Aquarian, to question all ideas and see if they stand the test of time or need to be changed to suit the present day. Quite the contrary with little Virgo, who just needs the facts in order to establish what's what and what isn't. Little Virgo's mind is excellent for the way Virgos live their lives but the Aquarian's constant rejection of established views will be disconcerting to say the least for this little note-taker.

...and now the bad news!

Although both of you have clever minds and shouldn't have many problem clashes, the area where things could go awry is the Aquarian detachment – reading Virgo's modesty as self-sufficiency. Little Virgos never ask for praise and will rarely complain if they don't get their fair share of affection. The Aquarian can quite unwittingly be a little cool and live life too much in the mind, and so neglect the physical needs. Virgos respond to plenty of affection and although they rarely initiate the cuddles they really need 'em more than most.

THE PISCES PARENT

The good news!

Piscean parents are gentle, loving, and devoted to the care of their children. Though rarely sticklers for routine their intuitive feelings tell them when and where the needs are. Pisceans play things according to the feel of the moment. This can make for sloppy schedules with any but a Virgoan child who, as soon as the communicative arts are mastered, will take over with the stopwatch. Thriving on regular routines and familiar habit patterns, this is one you don't have to spend half an hour calling in for lunch. Little Virgo probably laid the table and hinted that the fish fingers should be under the grill. Junior quickly gets the nuts and bolts side of this practical little life sorted out and with this parent the bonus of all that active Piscean imagination can go a long way towards expanding the sometimes narrow Virgoan vision. Virgos, though born realists, are often artistically talented and encouragement to indulge in some form of self-expression can sometimes develop exceptional talent. Virgos have the ability to work

intricately and meticulously so writing, drawing and craft activities will be greatly enjoyed. The surprising thing is that no matter how much activity goes on, little Virgo never seems to get into the mess that other children make. A nice bonus! The physical activities are great but don't forget Virgo's clever little mind. Good conversation, storytelling and writing will help to stimulate young Virgo's love of words and at the same time forge a close bond between parent and child. Never very good when it comes to discipline, the poetic Piscean will have little problem with these children who arrive on your doorstep completely equipped with their own sense of self-discipline, or at least that's how it seems.

...and now the bad news!

Piscean/Virgo rows could hardly be called battles – there's too much giving in on both sides. In a way this is as much a disadvantage as an advantage. Clashes will nearly all be about disrupted routine and bad timing but Pisces's loving nature is too demonstrably affectionate not to work wonders at smoothing little Virgo's frustrations. All in all this is a pretty easy relationship but it will be up to the sensitive parent to be aware of problem situations with this naturally reserved child. Encouragement to express feelings would be a great help to the sometimes matter-of-fact Virgoan so use your guile and plenty of cartoon comedies and weepies on the video. Share a box of tissues once in a while!

On the Cusp

Many people whose children are born on the day the sun changes signs are not sure whether they come under one sign or another. Some say one is supposed to be a little bit of each but this is rarely true. Adjoining signs are very different to each other so checking up can make everything clear. The opposite table gives the exact Greenwich Mean Time (GMT) when the sun moves into Virgo and when it leaves. Subtract or add the hours indicated below for your nearest big city.

AMSTERDAM	GMT +01.00	MADRID	GMT +01.00
ATHENS	GMT +02.00	MELBOURNE	GMT +10.00
BOMBAY	GMT +05.30	MONTREAL	GMT - 05.00
CAIRO	GMT +02.00	NEW YORK	GMT - 05.00
CALGARY	GMT - 07.00	PARIS	GMT +01.00
CHICAGO	GMT - 06.00	ROME	GMT +01.00
DURBAN	GMT +02.00	S.FRANCISCO	GMT - 08.00
GIBRALTAR	GMT +01.00	SYDNEY	GMT +10.00
HOUSTON	GMT - 06.00	TOKYO	GMT +09.00
LONDON	GMT 00.00	WELLINGTON	GMT +12.00

DATE	ENTERS VIRGO	GMT	LEAVES VIRGO	GMT
1984	AUG 22	11.00 PM	SEP 22	8.33 PM
1985	AUG 23	4.36 AM	SEP 23	2.08 AM
1986	AUG 23	10.26 AM	SEP 23	7.59 AM
1987	AUG 23	4.10 PM	SEP 23	1.45 PM
1988	AUG 22	9.54 PM	SEP 22	7.29 PM
1989	AUG 23	3.46 AM	SEP 23	1.20 AM
1990	AUG 23	9.21 AM	SEP 23	6.56 AM
1991	AUG 23	3.13 PM	SEP 23	12.48 PM
1992	AUG 22	9.10 PM	SEP 22	6.43 PM
1993	AUG 23	2.51 AM	SEP 23	12.23 AM
1994	AUG 23	8.44 AM	SEP 23	6.19 AM
1995	AUG 23	2.35 PM	SEP 23	12.13 PM
1996	AUG 22	8.23 PM	SEP 22	6.00 PM
1997	AUG 23	2.19 AM	SEP 22	11.56 PM
1998	AUG 23	7.59 AM	SEP 23	5.37 AM
1999	AUG 23	1.51 PM	SEP 23	11.32 AM
2000	AUG 22	7.49 PM	SEP 22	5.28 PM
2001	AUG 23	1.28 AM	SEP 22	11.05 PM
2002	AUG 23	7.17 AM	SEP 23	4.56 AM
2003	AUG 23	1.09 PM	SEP 23	10.47 AM
2004	AUG 22	6.54 PM	SEP 22	4.31 PM

John Astrop is an astrologer and author, has written and illustrated over two hundred books for children, is a little Scorpio married to a little Cancerian artist, has one little Capricorn psychologist, one little Pisces songwriter, one little Virgo traveller and a little Aries rock guitarist. The cats are little Sagittarians.